FLAME PETALS

SURYANSH S. CHAUHAN

ISBN 979-888546960-9

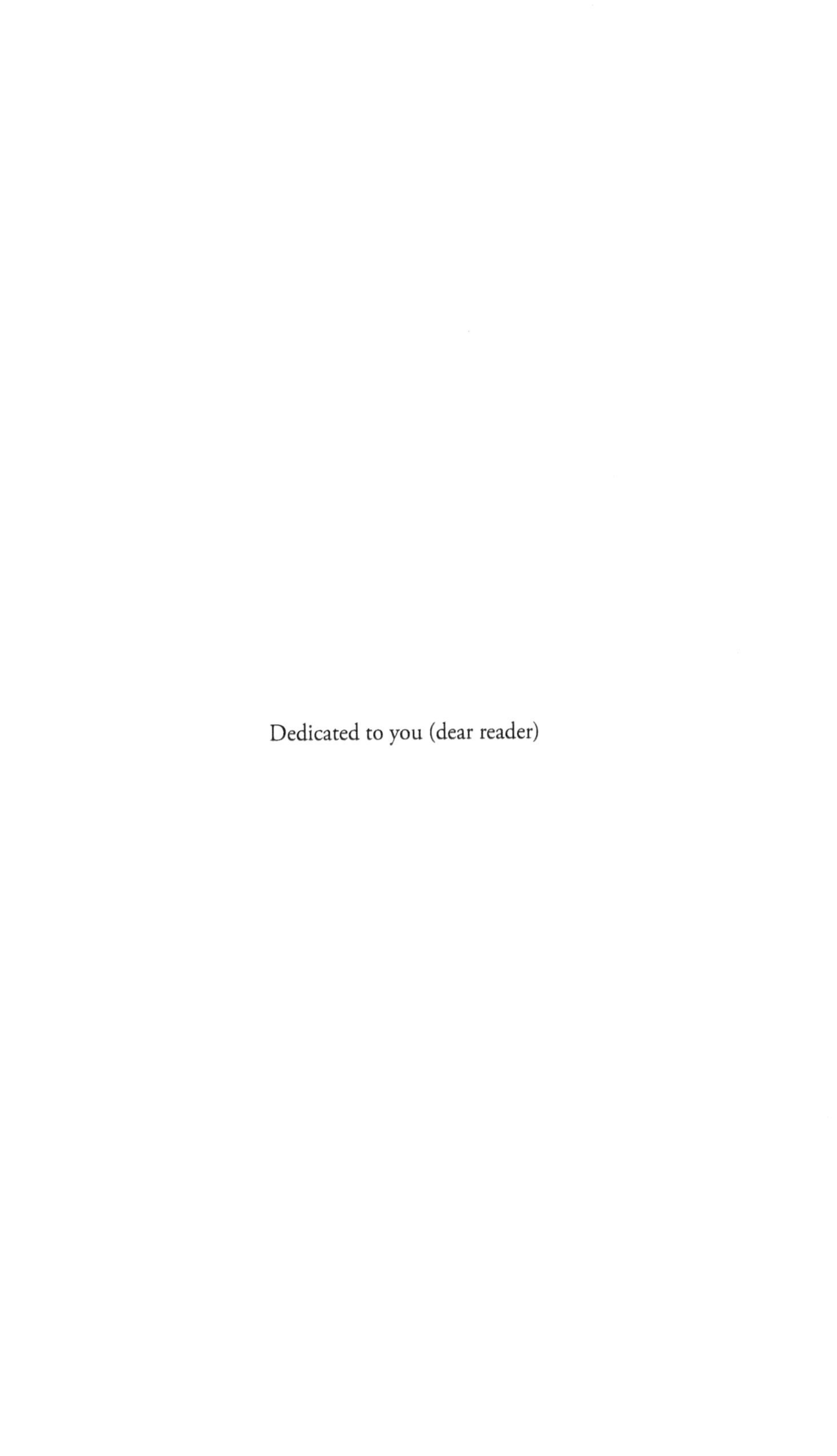

Dedicated to you (dear reader)

Contents

Contents

Contents

Copyright Disclaimer

This anthology is a work of fiction. All the poems and other write-ups are the original products of the co-authors are the products of the co-authors's imagination. Our editors have tried their best to check plagiarism in the content of all co-authors.

In case of any plagiarism, the co-author is solely responsible, and not the compiler of the publisher.

Preface

After being published as a co-author in 15 anthologies and a solo author, that too thrice in a year...here i am shooting my first shot at being a compiler.

I hope it goes well.

Acknowledgements

The successful compilation of this anthology would not have been possible without the hardwork and efforts of all the co-authors.

All the people involved in making of this anthology have devoted their time and energy for the success of the anthology.

I would like to thank my parents especially my mom from whom I inherited this skill and all my beloved friends, juniors and seniors for their constant support.

Prologue

Flame Petals

Petals that fall down with flames,

    burn before they even touch the ground.

    The concept of time is really weird,

    a blooming bud turns into ashes.

    The garden of words,

    full of beautiful poetry.

    All of it could be ruined,

    by the hate we hold within.

    To ease the pain,

    or to befriend it.

    We write,

    to fall asleep,

    or to stay awake,

    we write.

    With ink of heart,

    we shower petals of flame.

    - Suryansh S. Chauhan (Compiler & Editor)

1. Suryansh S. Chauhan

Suryansh Chauhan (going by the pen name : Suryansh S. Chauhan) hails from the city of Gwalior, Madhya Pradesh (Born : 29th May, 2004).

This teenager is a student at DAV Kota. Apart from writing, he also has a great deal of interest in painting and photography.

He's also a national level karate player & YouTuber for fun.

He started writing at the age of 14 and got published as a co-author at the age of 15 and then as a solo author at the age of 16. Debuting as a compiler this time. He believes that writing is all about framing one's own feelings, emotions or imagination in a way that it brings a sense of peace.

A lot of his poems are pretty long, simple and explanatory as if they're almost a song. He writes to express; for relief. Because he believes that art in any form is a therapy in itself.

Social Media—

Instagram : @suryansh_s_chauhan &

@thefadingbud_

Twitter : @Surya_S_Chauhan

Youtube : Suryansh S Chauhan

Mail : surya29.sc@gmail.com

Reciprocate

There's this girl,
Who told me
That I'm special.

But the distance
Is so disheartening
And I feel so terrible.

If the world was perfect
Maybe the ones we like
Would be with us.

Nothing could keep us apart
As we all deserve to be happy
And to smile wholeheartedly.

They wouldn't be so far away
Where we can't reach them
And the love ain't reciprocated.

When the lake of love
Reflects the Clair de lune
When the sea reflects the sky.

And the horizon disappears,
I hope for a world...
Where we could be how you want us to be.

But the reality is different,
You deserve someone way better
And it ain't me.

I do respect your love,
But I can't accept it...
As I can't reciprocate.

Sea Breeze

Through all these years,
I've been watching...

Hoping that you'd notice me,
But you're lost in your own world.

I want you to turn around,
And look at me.

Like sea breeze flowing
And playing with my hair.

Young love rejuvenates
Each time I catch a glimpse of you.

The melody gets sweeter,
And soft music keeps on playing.

I wanna dance across the streets
Blushing; weak in the knees.

All this time,
I've never felt no butterflies.

But you came out
To be an exception.

My heart skips a beat,
When your name pops outta nowhere.

My eyes find you
Even without thinking twice.

Maybe I am to blame,
For hiding these feelings.

But each flower blossoms,
At its own pace.

And the seasons
Keep on changing.

Yet here I am,
Treasuring the thought of being with you.

I don't know if it's love for sure
But what else could it be? I don't know.

I'm here on the edge of a rainbow,
Hoping to climb up and fill my life with colours.

But scared at the thought....
Of losing it all.

Even if i step forward,
Tomorrow is uncertain.

And today is temporary,
So what should I do?

Stepping into Tomorrow,
With or without you...

Reunion

A reunion,
In these rushed corridors...

All I want is
To meet those idiots

To relive those days
...just this once.

Tripling on scooty,
Going to school, less for studies
And more for meetups.

Planned bunks,
And classroom fun.

A small circle
But full of precious gems.

Hanging out whole day
And nightrides.

Group pictures,
Like time capsule.

Which remain
Unaffected by all forces.

It's rare to find friends
Who just get you.

A bond forged
through the years.

That goes on
Despite years of being apart.

When you all sit across-the-table,
And the nostalgia hits up.

And makes your world...
A little brighter.

Sea

Calm waves
And cold breeze.

Reflects the sky
And hides mysteries beneath.

Where land ends,
And the world seems endless.

As if the earth and horizon are one,
That's where lies the sea.

What's beyond?
Let's find out...

Set off a journey,
In search of the 'unknown'.

An adventure,
No one has ever been on before.

Changing shades of the sky,
From bright yellow to tangerine.

Let's forget everything we know,
And witness the world.

Let's set off,
In search of the unknown.

To unveil the mysteries;
Of the sea.

Flow Of Time

?Sometimes it's not necessary
for the past to repeat itself.

That's why, there's a
Forbidden scene with the same story?

Never-ending cycle without any brakes...
Holding on tight to stay.

But moving forward nonetheless,
Time stops for none and destiny still arrives.

For what tomorrow awaits is unknown,
And we're mere fishes flowing in the river
Who'd never dare to oppose the flow.

?The flow of time is old enough to break now,
But the fates of humans bind it for the perfect ending?

We'll fall like sand grains in an hourglass,
The strings won't split so easily.

As we grow,
we become more and more attached to this world.

?Memories we created were actually meant to left behind?

Like fallen leaves in the midst of autumn,
Covered in snow buried for an entire season.

But the snow will melt someday,
And the memories will come back.

Like a boomerang threw up straight to space,
Falling back with equal force.

And the memories will glow up the night,
Just like fireflies.

?Sometimes it will hurt,
But the wounds will heal soon enough?

With the warmth and joy,
That challenges the cold night
And the sorrow up untill now.

As long as there's someone who's thinking of you,
You have a home to go back to.

You won't be lost,
you won't be scared.

Just you smile and have hope,
As it can conquer even the largest territories.

What's meant to be may have no meaning,
But I don't care.

As I continue to believe in myself
and follow the path I've chosen.

(Suryansh S. Chauhan & Anushree Chauhan)

Hymn Of Love

?What will happen
When you will fall in love again?

But this time
More deeply and truely?

Will the movie be same as before?
Or should we expect a different ending?

?Doesn't matter
On which scene we will end up.

Until and unless your
Hands are entangled with mine?

And as long as I'm with you,
We can replay the climax again and again.

?Fits best for us,
Nevertheless our origins and souls?

Meant to be a blockbuster,
Just like I'm destined to be with you.

?Yes, the sky also
Laughs at us wholeheartedly?

The rating stars only go upto five,
Meanwhile we are under the starry sky.

Like glitter sprinkled all over,
Fate sure is a romantic drama.

?A clear lake beside us,
Singing for our love ?

Melodies that sound familiar,
But we don't know exactly.

And we're diving
Deeper every minute.

Even if it's falling,
I love it as long as I'm with you.

Being together,
Singing the Hymn of Love.

(Suryansh S. Chauhan & Anushree Chauhan)

Dizziness Of Life

?Have I been illusioned all this time?
'cause it was all blank when I realised...?

When I woke up to find
That my whole life was a lie.

?Maybe it was never
Meant to be found.?

And it was a worthless thing
To begin with.

?There is an uneasiness inside me,
Burning with extinguished flames of desires.?

Like a diary thrown in a furnace
And everything's burning up slowly.

Each page being slithered
And engulfed in flames.

?Leaving the cold ashes
As the only truth?

?How lonely the sky looks,
But I'm the one who found it more closer than the sky?

Maybe the darkness in the night
Is the real sky without any mask.

?If so...
Then my whole world is a lie?

Filled with false fragments of reality,
Fallen on my head.

And these pieces of glass hurt me,
Every time I try to walk away.

?And there I was searching for
The meaning behind my life?

But all I found was me
Lost somewhere without meaning.

?Felt like I lost my
Only sense of direction?

And all that's there is deception,
And I am no exception.

All I can do is wonder,
Why?...

?And I hate this moment...
May I should have never thought about this?

(Suryansh S. Chauhan & Anushree Chauhan)

Switching Lights

?Like mist over rose field,
Calling your name with love?

Like the last petal,
Falling over with a dying wish.

?This sure is
A sad love story.

'cause both of our wings
Were broken from the start.

We hoped our lives
To be like fairytales?

And when fire meets paper,
There's no poetry...

Only ashes
Which fall to the ground.

?But we switched our roles,
And turned to the darkside,

And now I'm the villan of this story
And you're my world?

You'd tear this world apart

Just to save me.

But all I want is

For you to be happy.

?Usakennai...

Is this reality we wished for??

A tragic hero with a broken love,

Isn't it too cliché?

(Suryansh S. Chauhan & Anushree Chauhan)

2. Anushree Chauhan

Anushree chauhan is one of the blooming writer among many flowers. She is a nature lover and animal lover. She loves to write poem which gives peaceful and fresh vibes. She is looking forword to give love and peace through her poems.

She has worked in many anthologies like Aakash, flower of light, etc.

Her hobbies are singing and sketching but she is interested in almost every things which amuse her and can make her mind engage.

She is a linguist, memer, humorous and loves to discover about different culture and traditions. She hopes her poem to be a peaceful sunrise for others.

• 24 •

A Lake Beside My House

A winsome moon in a living sketch,
Peach curtains flows like its breath,

Rent a house beside a soul blooming lake,
Night of stillness blends with its grace,

Moonlight enchant Lake's soul,
Feels like it's meant to be this way,

Ask the nightingale who witnessed the love,
Fir flies might have sent the words,

The lake must be indebt with the sky god,
Feel those longing vibes in silence play,

Rent a house beside a lovesick lake,
Night of stillness come for its sake,

Linked to my late night bed glory,
Near window of all imagination.

Brown Leaves

I can feel the air,
The winds are rushing,
Cold with a warmth of goodbye,

Old with a sense of beauty,
Raining over a stream,
Rustilng trees are alive.

Diving sun at the edge,
Greets and departs politely,
I'm grateful.

Old town hubbub, still so regular
Essence of each ally,
I'll take it with me.

Young guitar boy,
Two entangled hands,
Beautiful glare,

With the morning again,
With the air again,
With the promise again, I'll leave.

Blessing In Disguise

A hideous tree in a redwood,
Serves as a latibule to dove,
Tis so dern but still have a feyre soul,
It glows in dark shade and no doubt,
Tis a most hideous kalon home.

3. Ankita Negi

Ankita Negi hails from the picturesque town of garhwal.

She loves reading & writing. Besides this, she also loves basketball and firmly believes in self-love.

Instagram : btw_ankita05

Until We Meet Again

Those special memories of you
The moments we shared.
Even in the darkest days
We're strong because we're together,
Together we're strong.
But now when you're gone,
You are always in my heart
You'll always be.
Owning a special place,
That no one else could ever replace.
If only I could have you back,
Even for a little while.
I am ready to give my everything,
Because all I want is us.
Our bond, those memories,
Will always reside in my heart.
I surely believe,
Somehow, someday, somewhere
We will meet again.
Till then I am grateful,
Grateful for all the happiest moments
In which we were together.

What Colour Are His Eyes?

What colour are his eyes?
They are the color of flourishing vine,
Whose kindling cluster glow.
In his eyes,
I saw the colour of leaves.
Just like woods on a warm summer day,
When the leaves have just unfolded.
Everything looks so fresh and adorable,
His eyes are the colour of heavenly nature,
His eyes are 'Hazel Green'.

Would You Stay?

Would you stay as you are?

The guy I fell for and once knew.

If I didn't look the way I look would you still show your affection?

Would you just stay the night or stay forever long?

If I could no longer write these words of love?

Would you still be here?

If I showed you my secrets would you keep them tied to your heart?

If for one time I could not be brave?

Would your love still come wave by wave?

4. Aparna Sharma

From a very small age, she had keen interest in writing. She usually writes short stories, poems, songs and when she feels too much free, then ends up writing a novel.

Besides writing, singing is her other hobby. She has keen interest in History and Astronomy too.

Instagram : @__.c21y__

Mother and Father

Mother and father,
You're the feeling of God's Presence
You're the cheer of lovely essence
You're the frangrance of caring feel
You're the only reason of my zeal

When huge way of sorrow sea
Came to me as if it was some hell
You came to me as my beautiful heaven
And became my most protective she'll

When I won my first hurdle
You told me "Don't celebrate early success,
First victory does not mean that
You've got all your success
It's the life going on
Which will give u many test
Get ready for task of next
By a little work and little rest"

The sacrifice for me that you show
I can't repay any that very well I know
I'll try to know what you want so that
I can give you what all you expect

What you give in this all
Life isn't long enough to return that all.

Far Away From The World

So far away I want to go
Where there's happiness and no sorrow
I'm dreaming of that brightening light
Where there's all green and sunshine bright
Nature's beauty there sprinkles
Every night there Sirius twinkles
A place where is fun and joy
I can jump and dance, no one to to annoy
Where I can jump in wet muds
Where I can fly along with birds
I wanna feel that dreaming beauty around me
Where I appreciate this beautiful nature's grace
Where I needn't care about people
And with all animals I can have race
I wanna go in that beautiful dream
Where there's no sorrow
The world where's there only place
This world, Oh Lord, Can I borrow?

The Two Ways

Once I went through road of life
I saw two ways one left and a right
Everyone said to choose the left
But my choice was leaning to the right

One way was liked by others
And the other one was liked by me
I knew left one will leave me sad
And the right one will make me happy

When time was to choose the one
By hearing inner me, right one was chosen
And this was the one of my best choice
When I bravely heard my internal voice

5. Drishti Singhal

Drishti Singhal loves to read and write. She also has hobbies like Dancing and singing. She has previously worked in many anthologies like Hedging your bets; Unsung tales; Shine of love..etc

Instagram : @_drishti.ii_

Still

STILL

You broke me so easily,
Like if I was nothing for you;
You thought I'll move on easily,
Dude! I am asking my existence too..!!

Look at the past again,
How adorable we were together;
You were so precious for me,
I thought it would last forever..!!

Now, It's been a long time,
Since we met;
I trust my love for you,
And I am sure you'll regret..!!

I wish I could have more time,
To be with you;
Even though you left me,
But I still love you..!!
But I still love you..!!

Will You?

In dark nights,
Will u be my moonlight?
In colder days,
Will u be my sunlight?

In harder times,
Will u flow with my tears?
In alone nights,
Will u help in overcoming my fears?

In selfie poses,
Will you be my partner?
In the garden full of memories,
Will you be my gardener?

I dont want any expensive gifts,
Will you give me your time?
In my love poems,
Will u be my rhyme?

If I'll be the star,
Will you be my shine?
If I want to end this relationship with marriage,
Will u be mine?
Forever?
Will u be mine forever?

Soulmate

You are peace of my mind,
That comes from having pleasant dream;
You are my moonlight shining on water,
And warmth of sunlight's beam..!!

You are invisible circle of protection,
That reminds me that I'm safe even in the dark;
Our moments is the reason for my smile,
Especially those meetings in the park..!!

You are my beautiful thinking,
That comes from love of Darkness or night;
I m comfortable in that darkness only,
You won't believe that you are my love at first sight..!!

I love that hypothetical conversation,
With you my love bird;
Believe me you are my love at first sight,
You can't be expressed in words..!!
You can't be expressed in words..!!

6. Harshita Agarwal

She's a 16 year old and she loves to collect hobbies, including writing and reading. A cat mom who is still in the process of figuring things out. Even so, she can be annoyingly pedantic and cute at the same time.

Instagram : harshitaaawn

My Almost Lover

My heart aches;
with pain, because we couldn't be.
with fondness, because of what we were.
we didn't love,
but we had the potential to.
i don't love you yet,
but i would in a heartbeat.
the thought of our 'almost' makes me beam,
the thought of our 'almost' makes me lour.
we aren't nothing,
we aren't something,
we lie somewhere in between.
and for everything that we are,
i am grateful.
i am content.

I Adore You

I am grateful that you exist

your chocolatey brown eyes
your shy half smile
your flattering gaze
you're the one i chase
it's you whom i want to embrace

my heart flutters with joy,
everytime you say my name.
would you let me hold you?
would you let me caress you?
would you shy away from me
or would you let me embrace you?

No labels

No labels..but

can you love me without any labels?
can you care for me without any labels?
would you hug me when im not tolerable enough?
would you hold me when i'm just a broken glass shard?
are you willing to handle me?
are you willing to bear my silence?

even without any labels,
would you love me?

even without any labels,
will you stay?

7. Mumal S.

A day dreamer penning down her random thoughts and unheard stories , giving an insight of her own world

Email : mumals1130@gmail.com

When It's You

When I saw you , I saw myself

When I want you , I want you to be with me at that point of time

When I love you , then I don't love anyone the way I love you

When I talk to you , I talk to the love of my life

When I see future with you , I see the bonding between the sun and the universe

When I imagine you with another girl , I saw myself losing in this busy world

And like this never ending world , I have never endikng feelings and love for you

Lost

When ever I include someone in my diary , I lose them in reality

Whenever I feel like there is someone for me , I end up losing them

I included my best frnds, I lost them

I included my boy , I lost him

By including in my diary , I mean by thinking about them day and night

I connect to many, few connect with me back

I spend time with them then they leave me trailing back

It's been reiterated plenty of times ,

each time I'm hurt ,

I decide... not to repeat it

but I end up repeating it,

Everytime I'm writing is everytime I'm hurt. Whenever I'm hurt i write....

I write - not to repeat these mistakes

I write - no one is mine

i write - only I'm gonna be with me ,

but I just end up writing only

I never ended up implying them

My Euphoria

I don't want you for expensive gifts,

I don't want you for rare flowers, I don't want you for exotic chocolates...

I just want to cling onto you

As my anchor; as my constant

In the vertexes of these bleak emotions,
You make me laugh when I want to cry,
Make me smile when I want to die,
You've turned my life upside down,
Being bonded to you is an emotional bliss,
My heaven is in your arms...

Make me wonder when I want to frown,

Sitting next to you is like taking a sip of eternity,
When everyone else was gone; you became my home
You're my refuge, my euphoria...

8. Prajjawal Gupta

Prajjawal Gupta hails from the smart city of Kota, Rajasthan. He's interested in writing and reading. Besides this, he's a national level skater and his aspiration is to become a successful entrepreneur.
Instagram : @skateworld_prajjawal

You Can Do It

You can do it, you are determined,

You will be at the top and it's confined,

For success, he is totally blind,

Whatever it takes I never mind,

You are going to be good in life,

As you are kind,

And except you no one can break the limitations that you yourself has

bind...!!

You Are The One

Yes you are the one, who can touch the sky,

Yes you are the one, just stop telling lie,that you can't fly,

Yes you are the one just you have to rely,

Yes you you are the one with utmost potential,just you have to apply...!!

That's Me

I will write my own life's story,

I am in search of more glory,

I belive daring moves are far better than unwanted verbal theory,

I am going to prove all of them wrong who doesn't believe in me and tbh

sorry but I am not sorry...!!

9. Sakshi Sharma

An extroverted introvert who writes when she can't sleep! Pursuing English(H) from Delhi University, this talent believes that We are just stories at the end so let's write before life finishes its chapter.

Instagram : @sac.sheee

Windows

No doubt I own these windows of my room

but these Windows carries our memories fume,

The unspoken shades of dusk remind me

of you and me being together...

the shattered heart of mine tells me

that you didn't meant it forever,

I own the pondering silence of my heart

which experiences the thunderstorms of separation.....

but I know it won't be worthful to again start

except of collecting those heavy recollections,

the trees standing up straight towards there

still waits for the incarnation of our shadows...

the darkness that has absorbed the lights of my room here

still waits to glance for that serenity of the rainbow,

I sit for long hours everyday near these windows

experiencing the poundage of our reminiscences....

the way you, holding me in your arms

and leaving my hand within a second across that lane,

These windows listen to my pain

and yet wants to welcome you....

so I have decided now to put the curtains off

to give a start to my remaining life,because...

Sometimes falling can be a new beginning too!

superHEro

Wasn't that satisfactory?

wasn't that calm?

being holder, whole day

in his muscular arms.

Nonstop childish clashes with him

mixed with illogical curiosities

being answered, all the doubts,

asking me to face the realities.

Talking about the same hypothetical heroes

the ones: jumping,running, flying

being happy,day and night,

I wish I could learn from him:

how to put smile after crying?

Challenging each other with same tasks

rewarding together with comfy clasps

being rigid,for rest of the world,

I could receive all his warm claps.

Wasn't that you who showered the feelings?

wasn't that you who beared the pain?

it was just YOU who judged my potential,

and asked me to pursue all that...what all I can!

It is just an initiative by me for him

to pen down my feels altogether,

but I know this is the real fact that

no combination of 26 alphabets can define my FATHER!

UnderGo

You may find this place deserted
but it carries the evocation of our one time,
this room may seems sequestered
but it bears the input of my haunting crime.
The windows may appear vacant and uncovered
but it has engulfed my agonizing pain,
you may consider the curtains still
but they will show their substantiality, when it will rain.
Undoubtedly the zephyr has lost it momentum
even, the flowers have obliterated their gratifying essence,
The sparrow who was my diurnal visitor
has now started marking it absence.
You may examine this four walls covered area
inaudible, uninhabited and full of differences,
but once you undergo into its stillness
you will hear the walls speaking....
once the SILENCE SILENCES!

10. Sanskriti Saumya

Sanskriti Saumya

A passionate singer rising from the land of forests, Jharkhand.

Who is still a high school student and is working to shed lights on sensitive or unheard topics through writing.

Instagram:- @Sanskritisaumya_

Twitter:- @Sanxriti1

Success

SUCCESS

How far have you
reached on your way to the race?
Oh! Don't ever be slow or you'll lose your pace
There's a long way to go but don't get distracted
Your only way to success is focus more focus

Read all the books you can no practicals needed
They'd look for your degree not what you have learned there
Get straight A's forever you can't get a B
When your friends will be successful then you'll be sorry

You have your own dreams you can't persue that
These failing decisions will make you look back
You passion makes you happy is that all you want?
White diamonds, tall buildings isn't that what you asked?

So you see this race has been going on for long
If you are mediocre then make your heart strong
No room for passion or creativeness here
Cherish all the tiny things please don't live in fear

Anxiety

As the night begins
I feel like I'm gripped
My heart feels so empty
Like somewhere it has slipped

The fear of nothing
Creeps inside my mind
My whole body is fidgeting
But I still have shivers down my spine

They say its you should express your fears
But if I expressed they'd be mad
Because all fears are normal to them
But my anxiety makes me a maniac

Home

Walking miles and miles
To find a bit of peace
To find a spiritual space
Where there would be no stress

Walked for hours
A million of miles
What did you lose?
What could you find?

Stop for a second
And give it a thought
This home you've been searching for
Is way beyond

Endlessly searching for a place to find peace
Now you remember all the things that you missed
Skywatching,smiling or holding their hand
The home was always there that was the great beyond

11. Sanya Gupta

Sanya Gupta is a budding writer hailing from the city of Kota, rajasthan. She believes that self-confidence is her power to build herself.

Instagram : sanya__1613

Mysteries Of Life

Whatever is good for your soul, do that,
There will be many little things which you'll get.

Get out there , and live a little,
Don't waste your time in your own riddle.

Say yes, take risks, and live a little on your own terms,
because there are monsters like human spreading like germs.

There are far better things ahead,
You just have to wake up from you bed.

The Power Of Love

He shows his love which is naturally made,
The love is unforgettable which cannot be fade.

Count the stars or feel his love,
They are those which are mentioned above.

His scolds and the slaps we can't forget,
But that's his way which makes us perfect.

He's neither the God nor magician,
But still he knows all our communications.

He never showed me his love in an open way,
But he did all those things which could be remembered each day.

Dream

Could be the most beautiful thing in the world,
But it won't take time to turn into a nightmare.

An evil eye looks for me in the dark,
As I run my sight around the room.

The curtains wave and scare me,
The clocks create weird sound.

I hear footsteps behind my door,
I hear the shaking floor.

12. Satyam Kumar Choudhary

A teenager hailing from the land of five rivers, Punjab
Who has completed his high school and now looking forward to make
a career out of Writing.
Instagram?: satyamchaudhary22
Snapchat?: satyam271103
Twitter?: Satyamchy1

A Dream

The Garden is empty

There's no one around

Come down and join me on the ground

Let us make love

I will show you how

But hurry! Honey

I need you now

I saw this view in my dream

Which made my hormones scream

I kneel in the prayer

That one day we'll be there

I'll see the most beautiful face

Your body, totally bare and full of grace

I don't think it's real

It's all in my mind

I'll surprise you from behind

I'll hold you and cuddle

Stop me before I peddle...!!

That Night

That night,
We were all alone
Two bodies, one soul
All naked and I fall

Its not lust
Its not love
Its the fantacy of all

The warmth of two bodies
Heated up the doll

Nothing to do with sleep
Nothing to do at all

It was not her fault
Not mine
It was all about that sensual night...!!

I Love You

My vivacious whisper
in your ear
The people around us
totally unaware

You tremble at the power
of my words
I love making your body blush

I wrap my fingers
around your hair
And pull you near and near

My fingers wants to
touch your body fully raw
And let our hearts
have a deep convo

Eternity is a step away
My love continuous to grow
with each passing day

I've never get it before
With you coming near to me
I love you even more, more and more...!!

13. Sukant Shaw

Sukant hails from the town of Titagarh, Kolkata. He isn't pursuing writing as a career, he just writes whatever he feels at the moment. He belongs from a Middle class family or say lower Middle class family , so he has seen his parents struggle to make him educated. "When you realise how much your parents have struggled, then they are the only ones who become your inspiration. Just like that, his inspirations are his mother and his father. They've supported him through his thick and thin. Moving apart from that his aspiration is to become an Indian Air Force officer.

Social media id : __sukantshaw_

A Parent's Heart

When you feel like crashing in,
Who was there to forgive your sin?
When you cried your lonely tears,
Who was there to fight your fears?

And when it feels like no one would understand,
Who was there to hold your hand?
There are people whom you can't replace,
They are the only one who gave you face.

They will love you through thick and thin,
They show you light from deep within.
And if by chance you happen to die,
They will be the only one who will really cry!

There's no one who can love you more,
Than your parents for sure!
Always remember this is true,
Wherever you go your parents are for you!!

Life

Life is so strange
Nothing stays the same
Everything change
But who to blame

Life is like a game
Where you have to lose
Before you can gain
To win you have to face the fearful rain

You have to be strong
Stop doing the wrong
And never lie
Be ready for your last goodbye

Today you walk & talk
Tomorrow you lay in your grave
And nothing it gave
The money that you save

Only A Dad, But Best Of Men!

Only a dad,
With tired face,
Coming home,
From the daily race.

Bring a little of,
Gold or fame,
To show how well,
He played the game.

But glad in his heart,
That his own rejoice,
To see him come,
And to hear his voice!

14. Vanika Kaw

Drunk on my emotions,
Find me @vanikahahaha on Instagram

Lost

"I don't think anything compares to the grief of feeling lost. You don't actually know what's wrong, you can't explain what's going on in your mind and there's this constant ache in the middle of your chest like you'd just burst open into a million tears in the moment yet you don't know what stops you. One moment you're certain of everything in the universe and the next you just lose all your abilities to make decisions, you can hear your heart breaking, you witness your life falling apart, see the wretched pieces of your soul scattered all over and the worst part is that you can't do anything but sit and witness all the colors in your life fading, burning away. You're left with nothing but ash, colorless and dark and you feel it slipping it from your hands.

I don't think there's anything worse."

Rancour.

Coloured Lies

Living the dream, diamond skies.
Smoking cigarettes, burning lives.
Laughing faces, sipping highs.
Dead inside, I'm breathing lies.

Rancour.

Enough

Been a lotta things in my life, but never enough.

Rancour.

15. Vishesh Singh Bhadauria

Vishesh Singh Bhadauria is a budding writer who's also passionate about gaming and wishes to represent India on a global platform. He wants to inspire everyone and make his parents proud.

Instagram : @carnival_writeups

Waiting for Rain

Whenever she turned the pages of calander I asked,
Maa when will it rain?.

Preventing a child's feelings from being hurted,
She always used to say soon enough Beta just wait.

Even when it was the month for sun to rage,
I was waiting for Rain.

Whole year I worshiped the clouds to show their dark face,
Change of pages continued to take place,
But nothing came out which could satisfy my craze.

After a long run the time finally came,
The clander got torn off by wind's pace.

Tearing the leaves mocking at trees,
A thunderstorm came for an entire day.

Vidhyalay

I used to find myself near a lake,
Where I came every night to wash my face.

I never remembered did i slept,
Or did my body go weak and faint.

I wondered whether there is meaning in one's life,
Or I was only destined to serve these whites.

I never got the opportunity to read or to write,
Until I saw the footprints of the one's who were fighting for my rights.

Now I start by waking up to my mother's face,
I am blessed that I was able to match the pace of this great human race.

Now I visit this place which is filled with people who have happiness and
joy on their face,
My new home which everyone calls "Vidhyalay"

I Am Behind

I feel peaceful behind a clock's fingers,
Unless she turns into a top notch singer

My peaceful and sweet state,
Vanishes away from an exit gate.

I am Behind my inverted picture,
My face is even worse than a historic scripture.

My eyes which are meant to glow,
Looks like a disrupted river flow.

I am behind caffeine vapours,
Sipping the serum of anti vacation (coffe).

I am behind moutain of pages,
Wandering through the valleys of dark humanity ages.

Every mathematical odd and even,
Appears to me like a dark demon.

I am behind a suspens novel,
Adoring writer's use of vowels.

I am behind a colourful screen,
Three hours since there I have been.

I am back behind a clock's fingers,

Setting her up to turn into a top notch singer.

Previous Works By The Author (compiler)

The following books are a part of "Florio-Trilogy" by Suryansh S. Chauhan. Each book consists of 51 poems by the author :

• 'The Fading Bud' (ISBN : 9781639202218) 10th May, 2021

• 'The Evanescent Floret' (ISBN : 9781685236533) 11th August, 2021

•'The Dwindling Bloom' (ISBN : 9781685869939) 18th October, 2021

THE
FADING
BUD
Suryansh S. Chauhan

The
Evanescent
Floret

Suryansh S. Chauhan

The
Dwindling
Bloom

Suryansh S. Chauhan

THANKYOU FOR READING!